I WILL LIFT UP MINE EYES

"I will lift up mine eyes unto the hills, from whence cometh my help." Psalm 121:1 (KJV)

Lisa A. Carter

Print ISBN: 978-1-63616-204-1
eBook ISBN: 978-1-63616-205-8

Published By Opportune Independent Publishing Co.
www.opportunepublishing.com

Printed in the United States of America

For permission requests, please email the author
lacbook241@outlook.com

Four years ago…

the Lord gave me an interest in painting. I've always done some sketching, painting and crafting for children and youth ministry, but never any serious painting. I could definitely say that with this new interest has come some good therapy. I enjoy the creativity. It makes me smile, it expands my imagination and it's calming.

A number of months ago, He took my paintings to a different level and gave me a series of three subjects. When I received the first subject, I did not know there would be two more. I had no idea how to begin what He had given me. I know he has been teaching me as I go, and my paintbrush has been guided by His Spirit. I also had no real idea of what to do with these paintings as I completed them. I knew they were to be a witness, so I continued to ask Him to show me what he wanted. "I Will Lift Up Mine Eyes" is a result of those prayers.

In the following pages, you will find that each painting is accompanied by a story. You will also see that each painting portrays the same young woman in varying difficult circumstances. Although the young woman's identity is left a mystery; you may find as you read the stories, that you can easily insert your name into her life experiences. As the author of both the paintings and the narrative, some of my own story is intertwined within. As you read this book, my prayer is that the Holy Spirit will speak to your heart in every way He knows you need to hear him.

L.A. Carter

CHAPTER ONE
Lead Me on to Your Light

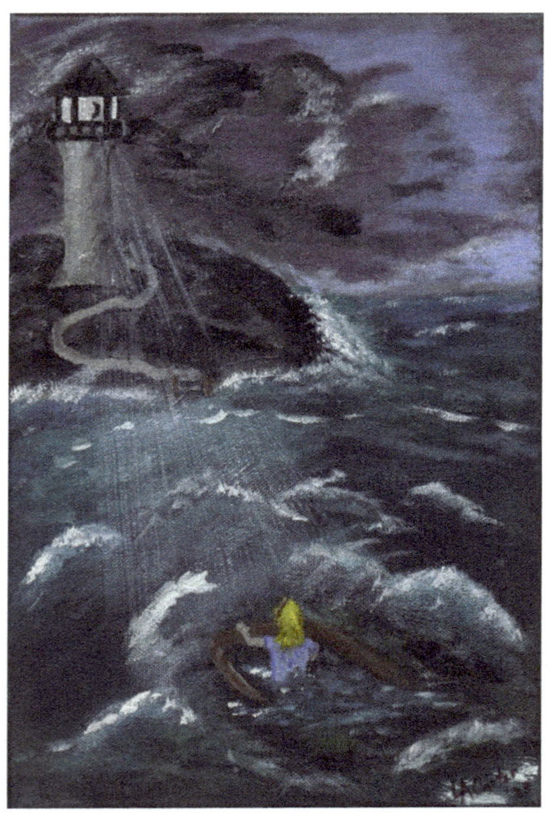

My initial inspiration for this painting was the lyrics to an old song written in 1932 by Thomas A. Dorsey entitled, "Precious Lord, Take My Hand".[1] Within the lyrics is a reference to a stormy night. It's a song about hope, strength and guidance in hard times. I think the subject of the painting is one that many of us can place ourselves in at one time or another. Maybe you are there now.

LEAD ME ON TO YOUR LIGHT
The Story

What began as a beautiful sunny day had now changed. With a worried expression on her face, she watched as the skies began to darken and the wind began to pick up. She had not expected anything but pleasantness from this day! She had been enjoying the sun shining down on her face. She had enjoyed hearing the sea gulls happily calling to one another as they skimmed the surface of the water and then soared back up into the sky. She even enjoyed sharing the lunch she had brought. Well, somewhat! You know how seagulls can be! She enjoyed the peaceful sound of gentle waves lapping the sides of her boat. It had been a very pleasant day up until now.

As the winds increased, the sea and the sky got darker and darker. The rain began to pour, getting in her eyes and stinging her face as the wind whipped it to the point of feeling like a thousand needles against her skin. Now she was close to panic as the waves tossed her little boat from side to side. "Okay think," she said. "What do I need to do?" She realized in horror that she had no way to contact anyone for help. No flares, no cell phone, no radio, and after searching frantically, she found she didn't even have a lifejacket. "Stupid," she said to herself. "I'm totally unprepared, well except for lunch and sunscreen," she thought sarcastically.

As her little boat began to take on water, she became terror stricken. She frantically tried to bail out water with her emptied lunch cooler. She just couldn't bail fast enough! The water coming in was much more than she could bail out! Gleefully, Despair began taking his hold on her as he whispered hopelessness into her mind, "You can't keep up! There's no way! You can't do this, give up! How long have you been out here? No one will miss you! No one will come looking for you! You can't stay afloat long! Your boat will capsize soon and that will be the end!" Finally, drenched, cold and weak, she did give up, and she found herself imagining her final moments. Despair and Fear had her firmly in their grip.

Time dragged by, but at least the rain had stopped. Still afloat, she held tightly to the bow of the boat as the roar of the sea pounded in her ears. "It's so dark! It's so cold!" she stuttered, as she closed her eyes and bowed her head to protect her face from the cold spray of the sea. Cold, dark seawater filled the boat and encircled her legs and waist like an evil hand closing in around her. "What was that?" she whispered. A distant memory pushed its way through her torturous thoughts. "Yes, I remember, from when I was a kid. Peace! Be still! Yes! I remember! Jesus calmed the sea and the fears of his followers when they were where I am now, and the wind and the waves obeyed Him. "Jesus?" she said tentatively. "Jesus?" She lifted her head, she gazed up into the dark swirling clouds, squinting her eyes against the cold spray of the ocean and cried out, "Lord? Lord Jesus? Help me too. Please Jesus! I need your help! I need you!" Moments that seemed like years passed. She lowered her head again; then a still small voice…, "I am here, Peace! Be still. I see you right where you are." And Peace began to wrap His arms around her.

She lifted up her eyes to the heavens again and realized she was enveloped by Light. Where was it coming from? She looked ahead and saw to her amazement, a lighthouse perched on a hill with a path leading up to it. Her boat was headed that way! This light was not circling around the area as they usually do, but was zoned in on her! Joy and hope filled her heart! "Oh, thank you! Thank you, Jesus! You do see me! You do hear me!" She looked around her; the waters were still rough and the wind still whipped, but in the midst of it, right where she was, He was! Despair and Fear had bowed to the presence of Peace, Hope and Salvation! As she rode out the waves, she was amazed that her boat had not yet capsized despite the amount of water it was holding. She watched the shoreline of the lighthouse come closer and closer. She rested in the warmth of the encompassing Light! Her eyes were fixed on this her Hope, Refuge and Salvation!

****

There is an unanswered question when we look at this painting. Did she make it to the shore? Yes friend, she did! Have you ever been in a similar situation? Have you been in a situation where Despair and Fear were speaking hopelessness into your ears? Regardless of how you got there, whether it was your own foolish actions or a result of what someone else placed on you, or just life's difficulties; you have a Savior who is waiting for you to lift up your eyes to Him and let Him calm the sea! Be assured, there is One that knows right where you are, Yahweh Roi, the God who sees you! Look up, call to Him! His light has the power to obliterate the surrounding darkness. His voice has the power to shut the mouth of Despair and Fear! He *is* Peace, He *is* Refuge, and He *is* Salvation. Life can be very hard, and we may have to endure some hardship; but there is a place of victory! There is a very present help in trouble! There is strength to be gained. Choose to lift up your eyes!

CHAPTER TWO
In the Cleft of the Rock

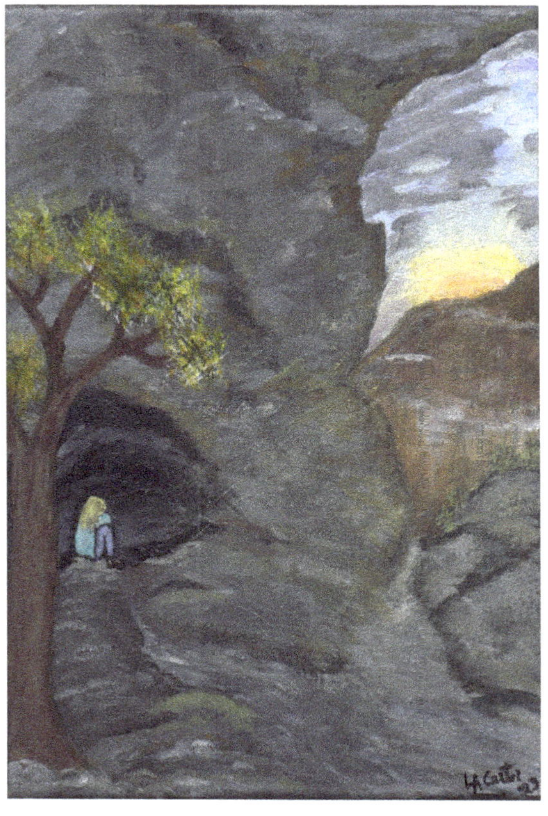

My inspiration for the painting entitled, *In the Cleft of the Rock*, was a song written by a blind woman who authored many songs. In 1890, Fanny Crosby penned the hymn entitled, "He Hideth My Soul."[2] This One who was her place of refuge, the One who hid her in the cleft of the Rock, was her constant companion even in dry and thirsty places. This One in whom she trusted, covered her with his hand, and when she was left exhausted and weak, He lifted the heavy weight off her shoulders.

IN THE CLEFT OF THE ROCK
The Story

The landscape was beautiful in its own way. There were very few trees, but there were a number of pretty, albeit scrubby, bushes. There were rocks and mountains on all sides, and each seemed to have its own personality of colors and textures. The beautiful blue sky above was only interrupted by a stray white cloud or two. She had hurriedly donned her hiking boots, jeans and a light jacket that morning; where she was headed, she didn't care. Life had pushed, pulled and led her in so many different ways that she no longer had any sense of direction. She was tired of being subjected to other people's demands. She was angry at everything and everyone.

She found a wide trail that morning that looked inviting and struck out to see where it would take her. She ambled along at a leisurely pace. The trail was not a difficult one, and as she continued on, it evolved into a deep canyon of lovely tan and pink sandstone. She walked along without much thought. She was just moving. She was just existing. She was just distancing herself. She wanted to leave it all behind: all the people who had failed her, all the hurts, all the losses, and all of her own failures. Sweet quietness is what her heart needed. As the day wore on, the sun began to slip behind the canyon walls, sweeping the beauty of the colors with it. Time passed in purposeless movement. The walls of sandstone around her were gray and black now, and they seemed to loom over her like phantoms. Phantoms that brought memories. Memories of hurt and fear began to flood her mind, and the anger began to boil up inside her again. She walked faster, as if doing so would help her outrun feeling. She wished for numbness and no feeling at all. She began to run. She stumbled in the dimming light, got back up and ran again, but she could not distance herself from the noisy persistence of those phantoms. Finally, exhausted and heart weary, she fell to the ground covering her ears in an attempt to shut out their constant barrage. "Why can't I escape them?" she cried. "I thought I could get away!" The cold of the approaching desert night began to creep into her bones. While Anger had abandoned her for the moment, now Fear and Despair tightened their hold on her. She huddled there in hopelessness as sobs poured from her innermost heart. "I'm all alone in this God-forsaken place," she whispered. "What am I doing here? Where am I going? Is there no place for me?" she cried loudly, her voice bouncing off the canyon walls.

Softly, a breeze began to stir through the canyon, and with it came a light, sweet fragrance. She lifted her face and inhaled deeply. "What is that? It seems familiar." She lifted her face to the breeze again as the fragrance danced around her almost as if it were calling to her. "Why is it so familiar," she asked herself. Gently, a memory came pushing to the forefront of her mind. "Grandma! Grandma always had that sweet scent about her." Her heart ached for the loss of her grandmother. There had been too many losses. "Why did she have to go away?" she questioned. "I loved her. She loved me, and with no strings attached. Why did you have to go Grandma and leave me all alone?" she sighed. The fragrance wafted through the canyon again bringing with it yet another memory. "Jesus loves you sweet child." Her grandma always told her that, but as she got older, she stopped believing. "No!" she would tell herself, "Only weak people need all that Jesus loves you stuff! I'm strong! I can take care of myself!" And, in afterthought, she would add, "I have to be strong, if I want to stay sane."

"Weak people?" she now thought. No one could describe Grandma as weak. She always had an incredible strength. What was it she used to say? *My strength comes from the joy I have because of Jesus.* Joy! Here I am out in the middle of nowhere, totally exhausted, totally lost, and totally scared. No Joy here! Another memory presented itself to her. Something about a shepherd who had lost a sheep. Yes, one of his sheep had wandered away. He cared so much about the one that he went out to find it, even though he had ninety-nine more sheep. That one sheep meant the world to him, and it was lost and probably in trouble. He searched until he found it and then brought it safely home. "Grandma loved me like that, but she's gone," she said bitterly.

As she sat there enveloped in memories, she once again felt the great emptiness inside. She had tried to fill that emptiness with lots of things, but it was still there like a deep black gaping hole. "Jesus? Grandma believed in you. Grandma knew you. Can you fill me up with the things Grandma had? I guess I'm a little like that lost sheep. Okay, I'm a lot like it. Jesus, I am that lost sheep! I'm lost. I'm afraid. I want a home Jesus. Can you find me?" she whispered. As she spoke to her grandmother's Shepherd, she lifted up her eyes and there before her, still to be seen in the fading light, was a shallow cave in the rock face. She slowly made her way up the incline and into the shelter and there she rested wrapped in quietness. Soon, she laid her head on her arms and fell asleep.

****

"Is there a place for me?" Have you ever asked that question? I have. Maybe not with the same words, but with the same longing in my heart. Many things happen in our lives that can cause us to doubt that there really is such a place. We experience loss that seems very unfair to us. We experience hurts that leave seeping wounds. These things and more, cause us to shut off feelings, stop believing, stop hoping, and dreaming, and then emptiness consumes us. We know the emptiness is there, so we spend a lifetime trying to fill it up. We try things that give us temporary highs, we try relationships with people who are floundering as much as we are, we try lofty ideas and philosophies. It seems, however, that at the end of each of these attempts, we find ourselves once again staring into that deep, dark hole. Is there a place for me? The answer is Yes. Truth is, we all need that place where we are loved, sheltered, cared for, and strengthened.

Like the girl in the story, call out to Jesus. Maybe you will say that you already went that route and nothing came of it. Maybe a thousand arguments will pop into your mind right now to counter any logical reason to try Jesus. Try Jesus. Talk to him from an honest heart. Share your pain, your questions, and yes, your anger. Ask Him to help you see who he really is, and what He longs to be in your life. Jesus told the story about the shepherd who went out at all cost to find that one sheep that was lost. Finding that lost sheep was the most important concern to the Shepherd; not all the circumstances that caused it to be lost. Jesus is that Good Shepherd. He has given his all to find you. He sees you where you are. He longs to cover you with his strong hand, and shelter you in his caring presence. He *is* the place for you.

Come unto me

*all you who labor and
are heavy laden,*

and I will give you rest.

Matthew 11:28 (KJV)

*He brought me up also
out of a horrible pit,*

out of the miry clay,

*and set my feet upon a
rock,*

*and established my
goings.*

Psalm 40:2 (KJV)

CHAPTER THREE
He Prepares a Table Before Me

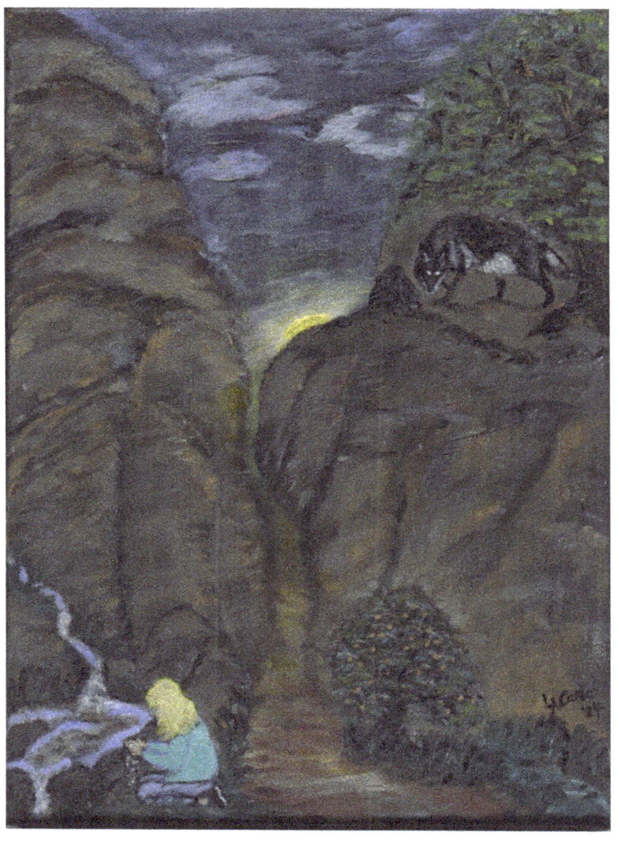

The teacher closed out the Children's church lesson that day as she always did, with a song written by Harry Dixon Clarke entitled, "Into My Heart."[3] I had sung this song with my class-mates countless times, but that day was different.

That day the words sank into my heart and I responded to the call of the One I sang to. The joy of my new relationship with Jesus Christ overflowed in my heart! Even as a child of seven I carried a heavy burden; but that day I felt so light and so free! When I returned home from church that day, I just had to share the news, so I went next door to my friends' house and told them all about this Jesus I now knew and how much they needed him too. That day I began a journey with Jesus, the One who would become my very best friend for a lifetime.

****

HE PREPARES A TABLE BEFORE ME
The Story

She had been following her Jesus faithfully! She had been rejoicing in his goodness! She had been growing and learning how to trust Him! She had been dancing on the mountain tops! However, now she found her path descending down into a dark valley of twists and turns. She was aware of an enemy's lurking presence although she could not see him. She did not want to be in this place. This was not a place to dance and rejoice! She looked to her left and saw huge boulders like the walls of a fortress spanning up to the sky! She looked to her right and saw more boulders with shadowy alcoves eroded into the rock face. "Is there no way out of here?" she thought. She looked hopefully behind her but only found more obstacles. She was hemmed in on every side but one. The only path forward was straight through the narrow, twisting granite canyon. The realization of this pressed down heavily on her. This was not what she wanted to do! It was as if she could feel, even smell evil hovering and watching from one of those shadowy alcoves above her. Little did she understand at the time that there was a spiritual battle taking place for her soul. Where was her best friend Jesus? Had He left her? No. He was right there to fight for her, to comfort her and to teach her. He was there for the long haul proving to her that His commitment was a sure thing. He would not leave her alone. A lifetime was before her of learning to trust this truth.

The stillness of the canyon was foreboding. She sat down and leaned against the rock face shivering slightly from its cool dampness. "What is happening?" she asked herself. "Jesus, are you here?" she whispered. She knew in her heart that He really was there. Ever since she had met Him, He had been with her. She knew that He loved and cared for her. However, her enemy's presence was palpable and she found it difficult not to doubt and be afraid! She had learned to share her every concern with the One who had become her Savior and her best friend; and now as she heard a deep growl somewhere above her, she began to do so in earnest! "Jesus, I'd much rather dance on the mountain tops! Why have you led me to this place? Jesus, it's dark here. I'm afraid! Don't leave me here!" she said as she closed her eyes and rested her head against the hard granite canyon wall. Only silence met her. Silence that seemed to last for ages. Then, a soft whisper like a melody, made its way to her heart:

> *"I am your Shepherd; you have no need to fear.*
> *I have all you need, just trust me and believe.*
> *I walk beside you*
> *To empower and guide you,*
> *And child, I will never leave."*[4]

"Thank you, Jesus," she breathed gratefully. The words of the psalmist David came to her memory like a witness of what she had just heard in her heart: *The Lord is my Shepherd I shall not want!* "So, Jesus, why am I here?" she asked. She looked in the direction of the path that would be her portion for a season. It still looked very dreadful! She stood, she squared her shoulders in defiance against the low menacing growl sounding above her, and she took her first step.

A multitude of steps later it seemed as if she had been walking this path forever! There were so many bends in the passage that she could barely see thirty feet in front of her at any given time. Nothing was sure, nothing was predictable and she was growing tired. The relentlessness of her ever-pursuing enemy was wearisome. Once again, she found her faith faltering. "Jesus, I don't know how I can do this! Why do I have to walk this path?" she sobbed in frustration. She began to stumble from lack of nourishment, and as she grew weaker, her opportunistic enemy eagerly lusted for the kill. "I can't go any further!" she cried out loudly. Falling to the ground, she curled herself into a ball and laid there as darkness fell. There, in that place, her faithful Lord covered her and gave her sweet, untroubled sleep.

Morning came. She shook herself in an effort to clear her mind. She looked down the path and could see the sun rising promisingly over a distant mountain. She fervently scanned the cliffs above her searching for her enemy. "Jesus, he's still up there following me. You kept me safe and you gave me rest, thank you," she said gratefully. She was still very weak and needed nourishment. "Jesus? I need your strength; I can't make it without it," she reasoned. The words of the Psalmist came to her yet again: *Yea, though I walk through the valley of the shadow of death, I will fear no evil, for thou art with me; thy rod and thy staff, they comfort me. Thou preparest a table before me in the presence of my enemies.* "You prepare a table before me, even in the presence of my enemy," she contemplated as she looked above her. "Yes, he's up there all right; but Jesus, you are here. You have gone before me to prepare what I need. Help me see! Help me see what you have for me even in this place," she quietly prayed.

She took a deep cleansing breath and lifted up her eyes to look around her. Little had changed, but just in front of her, a little distance down the path she saw a small spring of water coming out of the rock face and pooling into a little depression below. Directly across, along the right edge of the pathway, she saw a small bush with berries that she actually recognized! As tears poured from her eyes, she rejoiced in what she could now see. Not just the water and the food, but the evidence that her Savior was proving His faithfulness! "You *have* prepared a way for me! You know just what I need! You will take me through this, and you will protect me! However long I have to walk this path, however long I have to face my enemy; I know you will see me through it," she said with quiet confidence. Again, the One who had always been her best friend, her Savior, her Lord, her Jesus, spoke to her heart:

"Rise up child! You are in my caring hands.
Rise up child! Can't you see my promised lands?
Walk with me in this
I will sustain you
And child, I will take you through.
Rise up child, you are in your Shepherds care.
Rise up child. My goodness and mercy, follows you here.

When the time comes
I will lead you out
But child, you can dance even here. "[4]
And she danced!

****

Sometimes our Lord places before us a season of difficulty. Are you there? Know that His presence and authority is there to guide, comfort and empower you. He will walk with you through it and He will bring you to victory! Even in this place, His goodness and mercy follow you.

How do I know this? I was that girl in the story. I know what it is to walk through a season of suffering. My Jesus has proven time and again that He has all I need. He has endlessly proven His faithfulness to me. I am no different than you. He brought me through that season and He taught me along the way. He will do the same for you. Trust Him through it. Cling to Him. Walk this path with Him; He will sustain you. If He has allowed this season, He will not leave you to perish in it; but He will bring you out with great joy! Lift up your eyes, your help comes from the Creator of heaven and earth!

I will lift up mine eyes
unto the hills, from
whence cometh my help.
My help cometh from the
Lord which made heaven
and earth.

Psalm 121:1-2

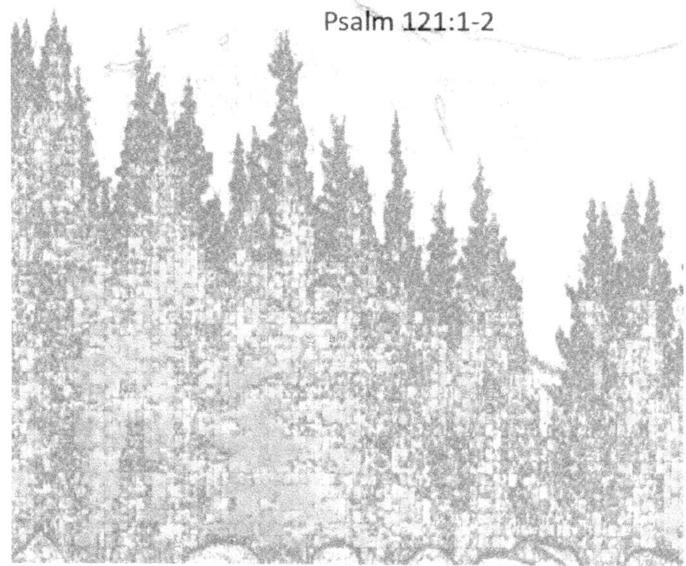

24

Endnotes

Artwork and Photography:
All paintings in this book are by L.A. Carter (aka. Lisa A. Carter).
Carter, L.A. (2023). Lead Me on to Your Light [Acrylic on canvas].
Carter, L.A. (2023). In The Cleft of the Rock [Acrylic on canvas].
Carter, L.A. (2024). He Prepares a Table Before Me [Acrylic on canvas].
Black and white photo: I took this photo while in Oklahoma at my favorite State Park. The lake is gorgeous and has beautiful cypress trees.
Modified photo: Before modifying into sketch mode, this was a beautiful photo that I took while in Colorado with three of my favorite people. They will know who they are!
Cover Photo: North Carolina Mountains by Bobby Collins

Songs and authors mentioned:
[1]Dorsey, Thomas A. "Precious Lord Take My Hand." Unichappell Music, Inc. (renewed). Assigned to Warner-Tamerlane Publishing Corp., 1938.
[2]Crosby, Fanny. "He Hideth My Soul." Copyright by Wm. J. Kirkpatrick, (Renewal). Hope Publishing Co., owners. 1918
[3]Clarke, H. D. "Into My Heart." Copyright: Public Domain. 1924.
[4]Carter, L. A. "Rise Up Child." Copyright 2024. A portion of this song is included in one of the stories herein.

Scriptural references:

King James Version, 1996 by Holman Bible Publishing, Nashville TN.

Acknowledgements

Throughout the unexpected adventure of writing these stories, different ones have been there to read my drafts and offer their insights. Thank you. It was a help in so many ways, and I deeply appreciated it.

Above all, I give thanks to my Light, my Refuge, my Shepherd, my Best Friend and my Savior, Jesus Christ.

Contact Information:
Lisa A. Carter
lacbook241@outlook.com

A Psalm of David.

23

The Lord is my shepherd;
I shall not want.
He makes me to lie down in green pastures;
He leads me beside the still waters.
He restores my soul;
He leads me in the paths of righteousness
For His name's sake.
Yea, though I walk through the valley
Of the shadow of death,
I will fear no evil;
For You are with me;
Your rod and Your staff, they comfort me.
You prepare a table before me
In the presence of my enemies;
You anoint my head with oil;
My cup runs over.
Surely goodness and mercy
Shall follow me all the days of my life;
And I will dwell in the house of the Lord forever. (NKJV)